YOU WANT PROOF? I'LL GIVE YOU PROOF!

"You want Proof? I'll give you Proof!"

More cartoons from

SIDNEY HARRIS

W. H. FREEMAN AND COMPANY
NEW YORK

Library of Congress Cataloging-in-Publication Data

Harris, Sidney.
   You want proof? I'll give you proof! More cartoons from Sidney Harris.
      p. cm.
   ISBN 0-7167-2159-7
   1. Science-Caricatures and cartoons. 2. American wit and humor.
Pictorial. I. Title.
NC1429.H33315A4   1990   90-39334
741.5'973—dc20

All the cartoons in this book have been previously published and copyrighted by the following periodicals:
Air & Space, American Scientist, Bulletin of the Atomic Scientists, Clinical Chemistry News, Fantasy and Science Fiction, Hipocrates, Johns Hopkins Magazine, Phi Delta Kappan, The New Yorker, Physics Today, Playboy, Punch, Science, The Scientist, Today's Chemist, Wall Street Journal, and a few extinct publications. The cartoons have been reprinted with permission, and our thanks go to all the above publications.

Printed in the United States of America

1 2 3 4 5 6 7 8 9 0   RRD   9 9 8 7 6 5 4 3 2 1 0

FOREWORD

By Albert Einstein

The following was recently found among Einstein's papers. Although the handwriting resembles that of the good professor, the fact that he has not been seen in his neighborhood (or anywhere else) for almost forty years leads us to believe that Einstein did not actually write this document. Thus, we request the reader to use her or his own judgement as to its authenticity.

This fellow Harris has been besmirching my character for years, while foisting off his skewed interpretation of science on the general public, and raking in untold riches in the process. In this volume, he tries to conceal his diatribe against me by carefully surrounding it with 118 cartoons of an irrelevant nature. He hopes the reader will be so confused by all the pseudoscience that he or she will have to undergo intensive science therapy, and not worry about poor Albert. But I will admit there are some things that I wasn't aware of—after all, how is a physicist supposed to know that steel wool comes from sheep, or that psychoanalysis came up the river from Vienna? Sigmund would have done anything to get some publicity, and hiring a river boat was completely in character for him. He never forgave me for using the term "relativity," and he wanted to trade me for it, but all he offered was a theory of dreams, a theory which was as unsubstantial as a neutrino.

The supposed revelation that I would eat two lunches in one day (not so cleverly disguised as a thought-experiment) is common knowledge to the regular patrons of Heinrich's Diner in Princeton. Heinrich—who we called Henky—would prepare such down-home favorites as Ulmburgers, Dusseldorf-fried chicken and beer shakes.

This was, of course, in the 1930s, '40s and '50s—before the introduction of fast food. If you wanted something in a hurry, Henky would give you a can of tuna and a fork.

In any case, the concept of fast food is very misleading. Until food begins to approach the speed of light, it can hardly be called fast, and there are so many obstacles in its way of achieving that speed, that at best it can barely approach the speed of taste. As for the quality of fast food, I have devised this formula:

$$Qf(X) = \frac{f}{x}$$

In other words, the faster, the worse.

The cartoon showing that I used my blackboard on which to draw caricatures of my colleagues is no revelation either. On days when breakthroughs didn't come, which was very often after 1915, that large blank expanse was very inviting. Besides, who among them did not draw caricatures of me? Madame Curie and her husband (we called him Monsieur Curie) once invited me to their lab to show me what they believed would make their fortunes: radium art. They had drawn a ridiculous caricature of me with a glowing moustache. I pointed out that a glowing nose would be more striking, but there is no accounting for Gallic humor.

Most of the science in this book is on very shaky ground, and I would hesitate to use it as a textbook under any conditions.

YOU WANT PROOF? I'LL GIVE YOU PROOF!

ORIGIN OF LIFE AS WE KNOW IT

"It's perfectly safe. If there's the tiniest leak, a siren goes off—a very, *very loud* siren—and everyone just evacuates the state."

BINARY LETTER FROM GRANDMA

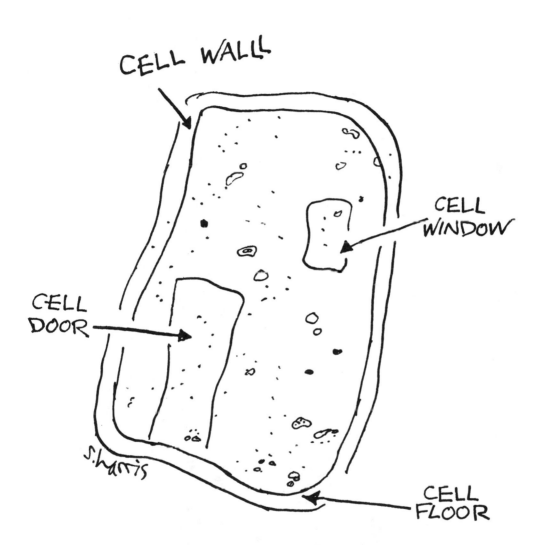

"Congratulations, Willis. You're being promoted to partially treated sewage."

"A wonderful square root. Let us hope it can be used for the good of mankind."

"Believe me, they're not expecting us. We're 387-year locusts."

"We sent a message to any extraterrestrial beings in deep space. It was picked up by an observatory in Great Britain. They didn't understand it."

"That's some of my earlier work."

A CLUE TO THE DOMINANCE OF MANKIND
WHILE EARLY HOMINIDS FASHIONED TOOLS AND WEAPONS,
EARLY CATS MADE RUBBER MICE AND BALLS OF YARN

"...so she tried to break into the father bear's computer, but it was too hard. Then she tried to break into the mother bear's computer, but that was too easy..."

"Attention—I'm having an endocrinologist in tomorrow to look at all of you."

"You figure it. We're naked, and we're not horny and we're not frustrated. They wear clothes, and they're continually preoccupied with sex."

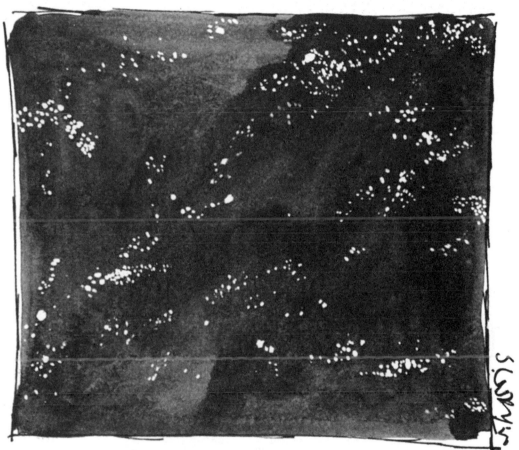

THE ENTIRE VISIBLE
UNIVERSE (DETAIL)

"What are we working on? I'm from Breakthrough Temporaries."

"The computer is claiming *its* intelligence is real, and *ours* is artificial."

"We're scavengers, we're ugly and we smell bad. If we didn't laugh, we'd crack."

"What's the big surprise? All the latest theories of linguistics say we're born with the innate capacity for generating sentences."

THE AGE OF REPTILES

3 years, 2 months   One minute   114 years

I.D. BADGE
AND SUMMARY
OF LATEST
ACHIEVEMENT
MUST BE
WORN

THOUGH HE CREATED MORE THAN 300
PRODUCTS FROM PEANUTS, GEORGE
WASHINGTON CARVER WAS UNABLE TO CHANGE
EVEN ONE OF THEM BACK INTO A PEANUT

"Schanz was a very great man. He was the first to say 'Feed a cold, starve a fever'."

HIGH-GRAVITY BASEBALL

"What I especially like about being a philosopher-scientist is that I don't have to get my hands dirty."

"The trouble with Mobius is he thinks there's only one side to every question."

"It's your computer. I'll have to call in a systems analyst."

"We couldn't get a psychiatrist, but perhaps you'd like to talk about your skin. Dr. Perry here is a dermatologist."

"With all I've learned about psychology recently, establishing who's naughty and who's nice is not as simple as it used to be."

"I've seen out to the limit of the observable universe, and believe me, it's no better out there than it is here."

"You can't build a hut, you don't know how to find edible roots and you know nothing about predicting the weather. In other words, you do *terribly* on our IQ test."

THE OLD SCIENTIFIC METHOD
Formulate a hypothesis. Accumulate data. Do extensive experimentation.
THE NEW SCIENTIFIC METHOD
Formulate a hypothesis. Patent it. Raise $17 million.
S. Harris

"This is the one—we want you to pray for *this* one."

"I'm afraid that dot matrix printing is beyond me."

"I guess I was attracted to particle physics for the usual reason. I like to work at home, and I have a very small apartment."

"The smaller we make 'em, the bigger we get."

"Dr. Birnes believes in the holistic approach."

"Don't mind him. As we take out the coal, he fills in the spaces with nuclear waste."

"What it comes down to is you have to find out what reaction they're looking for, and you give them that reaction."

MEGATRENDS IN SCIENCE

400 MILES

PARTICLE ACCELERATOR TO CIRCLE AUSTRALIA

CHIP NOW CAPABLE OF INFINITE NUMBER OF COMPUTATIONS PER SECOND

COMMON COLD VIRUS REMAINS ELUSIVE

J. Harris

"Krantz, you are being awarded the Dugwell Prize, for diligently working on one problem for 25 years without coming up with anything."

Leibniz, Boole and Gödel worked with logic.
I work with logic.
I am Leibniz, Boole and Gödel.
S.Harris

"We are nearing civilization—this is genetically-altered foliage."

"Think back—were there any musicians in the room when we operated on him?"

"You want proof? I'll give you proof!"

"Listen—it's psychoanalysis coming up the river from Vienna."

"Well, according to theoretical biology, it *should* exist."

"It's somewhere between a nova and a supernova…probably a pretty good nova."

Research Hand Signals

THIS IS GOING TO
TAKE ABOUT NINE YEARS

I THINK I'M ON TO
SOMETHING

WE NEED ANOTHER
#3 MILLION

WHAT I MEANT BY 'QUARK', IN FINNEGAN'S WAKE, IS A HYPOTHETICAL PARTICLE WITH A FRACTIONAL ELECTRIC CHARGE.
S. Harris

"Caution: This tomato soup combined with our chicken noodle soup can form a lethal nerve gas."

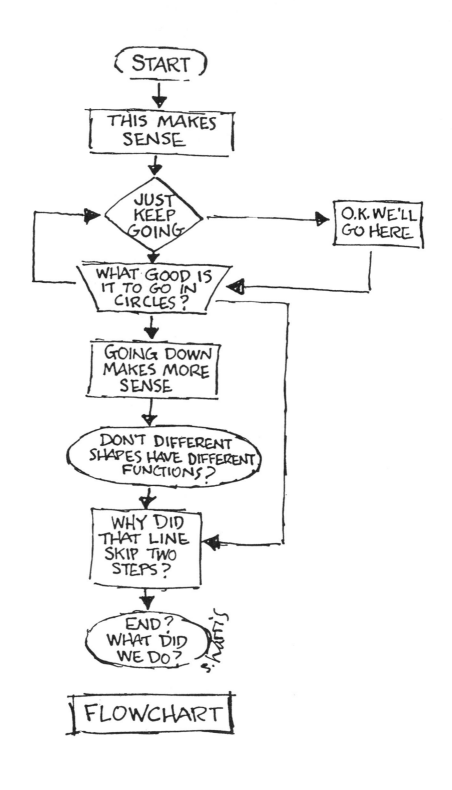

"When you awake you will feel fine, you will have no pain, and...oh, what the hell...you will cluck like a chicken for ten seconds."

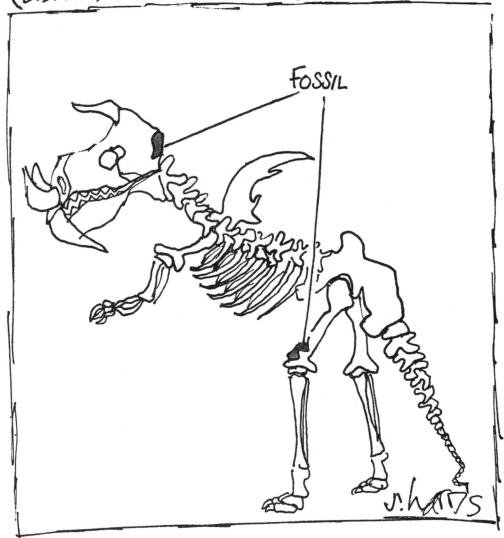

FOSSIL

"Ronald is *extremely* compulsive."

"It's hard to tell you this, Melnik, but you're being sent down to the Institute for Pretty Hard Thinking."

"But this *is* the simplified version for the general public."

"Coming to bat is Garrison, the shortstop. He's hitting .274, with 5 homers, his blood sugar and cholesterol are normal, and we're waiting for the results of his drug and alcohol tests."

IDENTICAL TWINS

KATIE M., BROUGHT UP IN FLORIDA, LOVES ORANGES, WORKS AS A BOOKKEEPER, ALWAYS WEARS SOMETHING BLUE, DOES NOT PLAY GOLF

ANNE M., BROUGHT UP IN LONDON, EATS FRUIT (APPLES), WORKS IN AN OFFICE WHERE THERE ARE BOOKKEEPERS, USUALLY WEARS SOMETHING RED (ANOTHER PRIMARY COLOR), NEVER PLAYED GOLF

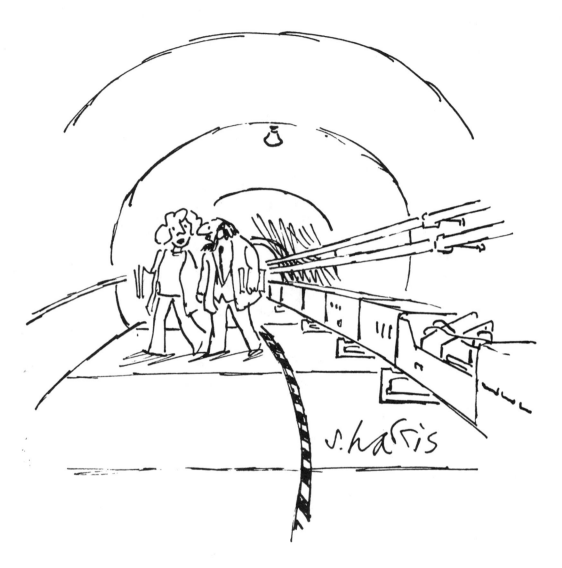

"What if we spend all these billions, and there just *aren't* any more particles to find?"

"I'm afraid I don't have a name. They've only discovered about half the insect species."

THE MAGIC OF PLATE TECTONICS

MONDAY

TUESDAY

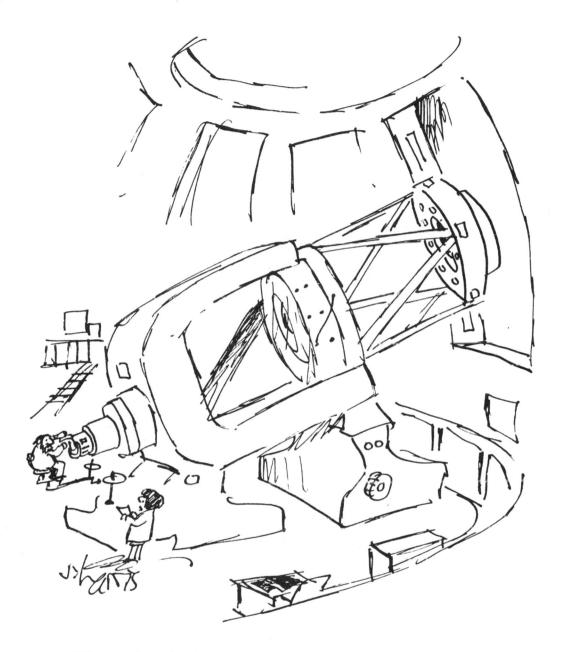

"The people at the Astronomical Society have already *known* of your discovery. They say it's Mars."

AEGYPTOPITHECUS

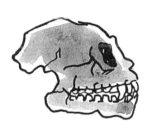

ATE ROOTS, NUTS,
GREEN SHOOTS,
INSECTS

AUSTRALOPITHECUS

ADDED MEAT TO
DIET

HOMO SAPIENS

EXPERT IN NUTRITION
   BRUSHED TEETH
TWICE A DAY.
   SAW DENTIST
TWICE A YEAR.

"These people were more advanced than we thought. Not only did they have the ability to make tools, they also made pegboards on which to hang the tools."

"It's a question of using the right metaphor. *That's* why the inflationary universe is becoming so popular."

"I'm not surprised about Methuselah. He was sick for over 430 years."

"Very creative. Very imaginative. Logic...*that's* what's missing."

"I'm on the verge of a major breakthrough, but I'm also at that point where chemistry leaves off and physics begins, so I'll have to drop the whole thing."

"We sincerely regret the unnecessary surgery, and we're going to put back as much as we possibly can."

"While we're working on the secret of life, Dr. Helmholz, there, is trying to unravel its meaning."

"It turned out there just wasn't any ordinance *against* strip mining on this street."

"This is a lovely old song that tells of a young woman who leaves her little cottage, and goes off to work. She arrives at her destination, and places some solid NH_4HS in a flask containing 0.50 atm of ammonia, and attempts to determine the pressures of ammonia and hydrogen sulfide when equilibrium is reached...."

"If it does collapse into itself, it will be the last word on contemporary packaging: the disposable universe."

"You can't imagine how tight our budget is. We can only work with single-digit numbers."

THAT SPECIAL GIFT FOR MATHEMATICIANS

4TH ANNIVERSARY

TETRAHEDRON PAPERWEIGHT

12TH ANNIVERSARY

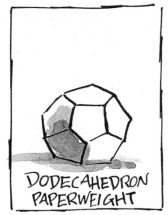

DODECAHEDRON PAPERWEIGHT

20TH ANNIVERSARY

ICOSAHEDRON PAPERWEIGHT

S LARGS

"What's going on here? What *you* see is what *I* get, and what *I* see is what *you* get."

THE SHROUD OF LONDON
BEARS THE LIKENESS OF ISAAC NEWTON
AND HAS A TENDENCY TO FALL TO THE GROUND

EINSTEIN CONDUCTS A THOUGHT-EXPERIMENT

ANTON VAN LEEUWENHOEK, THE FIRST PERSON TO SEE ANIMALCULES THROUGH A MICROSCOPE, DOESN'T AT ALL LIKE WHAT HE SEES
YECCCHH.
S. Harris

"No wonder he never forgets. He has a bubble memory with a storage capacity of 360 megabytes."

THOMAS EDISON RECEIVES HIS FIRST ELECTRIC BILL

"Landfill to the left of us, landfill to the right of us…."

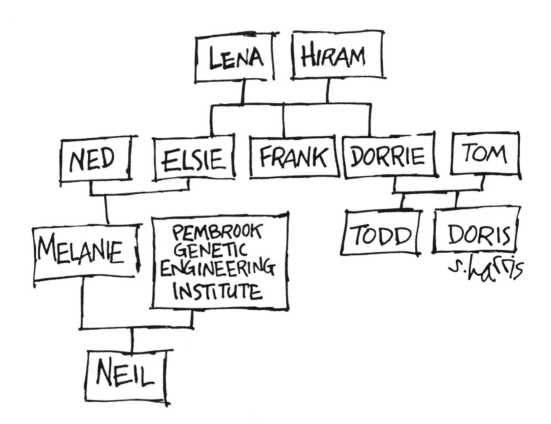

THE GEOMETRY OF EVERYDAY LIFE

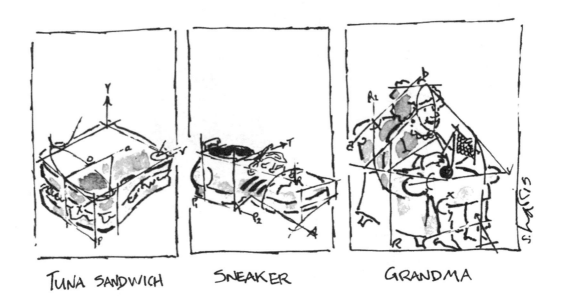

TUNA SANDWICH   SNEAKER   GRANDMA

"Is that *it*? Is that the *big bang*?"

"He was very big in Vienna."

"You're being recalled—He's going to try mammals."

"Now that we've come up with a sweetener 650 times sweeter than sugar, we're working on a sourer 475 times sourer than a lemon."

JOHANNES KEPLER'S UPHILL BATTLE

"I had a better grasp of things when physics dealt mostly with falling bodies."

"Roger doesn't use the left side of the brain *or* the right side. He just uses the middle."

DR. UNZIMER'S MOTHER APPEARS...
TEDDY, YOU CALL THIS A 'CLEAN ROOM'?
S. HARRIS

"Hedley got his training in ornithology, but I wonder if he shouldn't have been a grocer."

"Yes, this certainly *is* a highly polluted piece of air."

"Sure it beats walking, but we'll never get there."

"It's black, and it looks like a hole. I'd say it's a black hole."

HUNTER-GATHERERS, NORTH AMERICA, LATE 20TH CENTURY

"Recently I've had a lot of trouble conceptualizing any number larger than a million trillion billion."

"I hope we get to communicate with them—I'd just like to tell them we have no interest in communicating with them."

"But don't you see, Gershon—if the particle is too small and too short-lived to detect, we can't just take it on faith that you've discovered it."

"If a day is a week here, and a month is a day, and a year is an hour, how are they going to figure our pay?"

"Well, this should give us some valuable insight into the origin of the universe."